BATTLE
OF THE
NEW ERA

GEORGE WALKER

authorHOUSE®

AuthorHouse™ UK
1663 Liberty Drive
Bloomington, IN 47403 USA
www.authorhouse.co.uk
Phone: 0800.197.4150

Published by AuthorHouse 04/23/2019

ISBN: 978-1-5462-9810-6 (sc)
ISBN: 978-1-5462-9811-3 (e)

Print information available on the last page.

Any people depicted in stock imagery provided by Getty Images are models,
and such images are being used for illustrative purposes only.
Certain stock imagery © Getty Images.

This book is printed on acid-free paper.

Because of the dynamic nature of the Internet, any web addresses or links contained in
this book may have changed since publication and may no longer be valid. The views
expressed in this work are solely those of the author and do not necessarily reflect the
views of the publisher, and the publisher hereby disclaims any responsibility for them.

NOTE

In order to better your understanding, I have had these articles translated from Chinese to English, as you will see, but I have not fact-checked the translated material because of my limited level of English. The English version may not correctly express my original meaning, so it is just for your reference. For the original meaning of the articles, refer to the Chinese version.

FOREWORD

Battle of the New Era is a series of books; this book is book 1, and this book is the manual of the series of books.

In the book of Revelation, the term "battle of the new era" refers to the day when God dispatches a messenger to judge humans and their crimes.

Some friends ask me why I would title the book *Battle of the New Era*. I'd like to tell them a great deal in reply, but I don't dare, as a person in China will get into big trouble if he reveals the secret that God has asked him to do something.

Battle of the New Era was first published in 2016, and I have been publishing articles online for fifteen years. Many readers think these articles are vulgar and insensitive because they do not know my real intention.

It is normal for readers to think such a thing. How can one understand the depth of an article if one does not know how to read and view the values expressed in these articles?

It can be said that no one yet has truly understood my intention for writing these articles or each article's immeasurable value—a value not measurable in money.

When you finish reading *Battle of the New Era*, you will understand how I complete the mission entrusted to me by God and save the world by writing articles. You will see that I write articles and send them to the governments of different countries, ultimately changing world politics magically.

These articles are not myths but real incidents. All articles and incidents in *Battle of the New Era* can be fact-checked. I welcome all readers to investigate and verify, I can even help you do this.

Believe it or not, I am the messenger sent by the God to save the world in the end and judge humans for their crimes.

PREFACE

George Walker, the author of *Battle of the New Era*, has felt since he was young that his views are different from those of others. Mr Walker believes that God has inspired him to do something for humankind, namely to tell people what is right and what is wrong.

In 2004, George Walker put forward a reform plan for Chinese state-owned enterprises when China was going to sell out its state-owned enterprises and privatize them entirely. Mr Walker's reform plan was recognized and implemented by the central government, thus not only saving the Communist Party of China from collapse but also helping China's national governance get back on the right track. The national governance plan Walker had designed is still in use.

In October 2004, Walker sent articles to many Taiwanese legislators urging them to abandon an arms purchase proposal whose value was greater than six hundred billion Taiwanese dollars and designated representatives to engage in peace talks with lawmakers from the mainland. Chen Shui-bian stepped down and was imprisoned, and the Kuomintang came to power. Mr Walker even stopped the Taiwan Strait war, supported by the United States, in 2004 and saved humankind from disaster.

From that point forward, Mr Walker came to know that he is a person with great influence and a great sense of responsibility. It is his duty to present his opinion to China's leaders. No one can take his place and put forward the right opinions to the country's lawmakers. China's top leaders trusted him because he saved them by writing several articles and designing a reasonable plan for them.

In this unbelievable book by George Walker, he describes how he was called by God to compose and publish articles online.

His opinions and suggestions reverse political tendencies around the world, dispelling evil, terrorism, injustice, and demons, and usher in a new order.

Most incredibly, everything he writes about comes true, or is about to come true, no matter how inconceivable.

Some of the events that George predicted that indeed came to pass include Donald Trump's election, objections to North Korea, opposition to Islam extremism, and the reform of state-owned companies in China.

Called "a diary written to God, accusing all the world", George's revelations and predictions are astounding to behold and may actually reveal for the first time God's opinions.

CONTENTS

PART I

THE STORIES BEHIND BATTLE OF THE NEW ERA

September 2018

I write this story about the Centuries Sentence. These are true stories about my life, and all of the people involved in the story, except my grandmother, are still alive. If you are interested, you can seek them out to verify my claim.

I think this story is more attractive than the one about the battle of the new era, which enables people to better understand the book *Battle of the New Era*.

MY GRANDMA AND I

When my father was a teenager, he left Shanghai for Xinjiang to work as an accountant in order to support the construction that was being undertaken at Xinjiang.

My mother was born in Henan and worked as a farmer in Xinjiang. After retirement, my parents went back to Shanghai. Now, they are leading their retired life in Shanghai.

I was born in Xinjiang. My grandma had five children: three sons and two daughters. I am the only boy in the family in my generation. I have female cousins but no male cousins. It can be said that all yang qi of my family is concentrated on me. According to traditional Chinese culture, I am the only person who belongs to the Walker family. I am the only one whose children will bear the family name of Walker. And after my female cousins get married, they will belong to other families whose children won't have the family name of Walker. Therefore, they are not members of the Walker family.

So my grandma liked me very much and thought that I was the only successor of the Walker family. When I was six months old, my grandma took me to Shanghai from Xinjiang. I lived with my grandma since I was little.

I studied in a primary school in Beijing when I was in first and second grades. My older female cousin also studied in that school. I studied in a Shanghai primary school when I was in third grade. I studied in Xinjiang from fourth grade to ninth grade. When I was in ninth grade, I went back to Shanghai according to the policy at that time. Afterwards, I entered high school and, later, college in Shanghai.

My grandma was the person who loved me most. She left everything, including her house, to me.

But my grandma was most strict, particularly with others. She was the highest authority in my family.

My grandma used to beat me with a feather duster and other objects. I have forgotten what mistakes I'd made. I had obeyed her words since I was little, but she still beat me over trivial matters.

My grandma used to point out to me, with tears in her eyes, "Be a good person. Never be a bad person."

I feel I have mental diseases owing to the harm she brought upon me, which can be called "good person paranoia". I have been telling myself, *Be a good person. Never be a bad person.*

That is why I wrote this book. I should be a good person and not a bad person. I have suffered a lot. I have been wondering why a good person would be treated the way my grandma treated me. I have been making complaints to God. Why does the world treat good people like that? I accused God of all the unfair things in the world and demanded that he answer me.

I will prove to God that his past sayings are all wrong. I want to accuse the whole world.

My book records the communication between God and me, including God's answers.

I HAVE BEEN PROVING MY CORRECTNESS SINCE I WAS LITTLE

I had two discussions with my physics teachers about exercise when I was in middle school and high school. I finally achieved academic victory. All my classmates corrected my academic problem.

3

I know I have different understandings than others have. I am the only person whose viewpoints are correct.

My second-oldest uncle is a book lover. He is a common worker, but he has many books. Sometimes, I would take a few books from him.

I have read many ancient texts, including the Diamond Sutra, the Bible, the Tao Te Ching, the Koran, the Yellow Emperor's Inner Canon, *Capital*, and *The Selected Works of Mao Zedong*. Except for the Book of Changes, I could discern the authors' intentions easily. But ordinary people tend to misunderstand the intentions of the authors, which leads to serious social problems.

Those books, including ones about communism and capitalism, are instructions from God. And people's misunderstanding of the major problems laid out in the books leads to serious social conflicts.

After reading those books in high school, I gradually understood the main viewpoints and the authors' intentions through subsequent social practice. I gradually figured out the root causes of the social conflicts of the times and their solutions.

THE TIANANMEN INCIDENT, 1989

When I was in high school in 1989, there was a democratic movement called the June 4 Rebellion in China. It was the most important democratic event, and the largest social conflict, in modern Chinese history.

At that time, I was a good student and an absolutely good person.

Mao Zedong claimed that he supported democracy. Students' movements are positive examples of opposing feudalism and oppression, or so it is said in Chinese textbooks. It was the May Fourth Movement that led to the success of the Communist Party. That is what is said in our textbooks.

So I think that the student protesters were correct in what they'd done and had acted in a positive manner. But according to what we were taught in school at that time, the Communist Party and the country, not the student protesters, were correct.

We'd been taught that it was the Communist Party who had freed people from oppression. Communism, we were told, achieves social fairness, justice, and resource sharing. That is definitely correct. But the two camps of social thinking had a serious conflict on June 4.

I saw the protesters beat a few soldiers to death and burn their bodies. That image will retain in my mind forever.

What happened to Chinese society? Why had such a serious social conflict developed? That is a problem I have been thinking about.

After the Tiananmen Square incident, I entered a college. I thought too much, and my thinking was out of control. I could not stop thinking no matter if it was daytime or night-time. I could not hear what my teachers were talking about in class.

The situation became more and more serious, and many different thoughts gushed from my brain. In one midterm examination period, I failed in almost all my courses. According to the provisions of the school, I was required to drop out. At the last moment, I went to my dean for help. After learning about my situation, he suggested that I to go see a neurologist for a physical examination.

I was diagnosed with serious neurasthenia. The doctor suggested that I take one year off from school. By following his advice, I avoided dropping out.

For the rest of my problems, I asked a qigong master for help. An amazing thing happened after I began practising qigong. I felt I could control my previously unstoppable brain, and my body was restored to balance. But I still felt fatigued frequently and could not focus. After writing an article or reading a few pages, I would be tired and wanting to sleep.

I HAD A TOTAL 0.17 MILLION YUAN OF DEBT AFTER GRADUATION OWING TO BUSINESS FAILURE

I graduated in 1995. I wanted practice with people and contact with society, so I found some jobs related to promotion. I worked as a cemetery salesman, a food salesman, an office equipment salesman, an office equipment repairman, the boss of a public telephone company, a trainee of art wares, the boss of a printing shop, and a leafleter.

I worked hardest when I was a promotion worker. At one of my jobs in promotion, I biked twelve hours every day. After I'd finished with that job, I learned how to repair copiers and other office equipment and worked as a copier repairman, which was a popular industry at that time.

Afterwards, I founded an office equipment company with others. One year later, I registered a company and became the boss. That was the beginning of a nightmare. Because I always required myself to be a good person, I treated my workers very well, providing them with food and board and teaching them techniques and promotion skills. I trained them every day. But after mastering the techniques, they quit their jobs and founded their own companies. And they grabbed my clients.

At that point I would recruit more workers. I would teach them techniques and promotion skills and train them every day. After mastering techniques and sales skills, all of them founded their own businesses.

Soon I ran out of money. I borrowed 20,000 renminbi (RMB) from my grandma, RMB 20,000 from my aunt, more than RMB 100,000 from my friends, and RMB 30,000 from other source.

At that time, I was the president of the Huangpu Military Academy in the printing industry in Shanghai. After learning techniques and sales skills and learning how to get customers, my students left me, bought house and cars, got married, and bore children. But I had a debt of RMB 170,000. Fifteen years later, I sold the house that my grandma had left me, then I paid off my debt.

Time went fast. I only had RMB 2,000 in my pocket and the debt of RMB 170,000.

MY TEARFUL FAREWELL TO MY EX-WIFE

At that time, I had no options and thought only how to solve my dilemma. Then I came up with a good idea—marriage.

Since back then I was a handsome thirty-year-old man, I decided to post a marriage-seeking and recruitment advertisement.

The advertisement was rather attractive: "A thirty-year-old employer in a private company with house and property seeks to recruit an assistant and seeks a marriageable mate immediately."

Many people came to me for a time, but I did not like any of them. But then one morning when we had a company meeting, a young woman pushed the door to come inside and asked us whether the company was currently recruiting assistants. That young woman later became my wife (and later still became my ex-wife).

She smiled at me. I asked her to sit down, and then I drove others out the door. I spoke with this young woman.

From the conservation, I learned that her family also did business and that she herself was from a noble family in the imperial lineage of the former Qing dynasty. In the past, she would have been called a princess. In addition, she was still a virgin.

I thought that probably she was the right one for me. Given that she used to be an employer, she could help me better organize my company. By virtue of the power of her family, I could more easily get along with people inside the company. Actually, she also had superior qualities in many other respects. I liked her very much, and I saw in her eyes that she also had love for me.

We had a rapidly moving love affair and got married lightning-fast. As said by one of my apprentices, "We all knew that you were about to get married, but we still feel surprised at this. We originally thought that you might get married after several months."

My fiancée and I indeed astonished everyone.

My wife loved me very much. When I had been acquainted with her for three days, I asked her to help me manage my corporation's finances and gave all my money to her—RMB 1,200. She was rather surprised that the company had such a small amount of funds, but she did not look down upon me.

When I run across a woman who really loves me, she cannot refuse me. Therefore, this young woman and I quickly fell in love with each other. We dined together, walked in the garden together, and chatted with each other. A few days after we'd met, we had sexual relations and announced that we were engaged to be married.

Do not think that I am telling a pornographic story? Actually, this is a very cruel tragedy.

I ran across a woman who loved me very much, and we got married and continued to love each other. But three years later, in order to write this book and finish the mission God had given me, I abandoned my wife. We eventually bid farewell to each other in tears.

When I got married, my business took an upwards turn and realized substantial profits. However, three months after our marriage, I was suddenly arrested by police in Shanghai.

In addition to the debt of RMB 170,000, I owed RMB 200 to the telephone company. The telephone company demanded that I repay RMB 900, which included a large penalty for the bill's being overdue, one year later. I thought it rather irrational, and more importantly, I did not have RMB 900 available. Consequently, the telephone company filed a lawsuit against me, and the court ordered me to repay the charge. But I'd refused the sentence.

Therefore, the court dispatched two policemen to arrest me. They took me to the detention house. I will not forget my day in the detention house.

When I stepped into the room, the person in charge immediately asked me why I had been arrested. I smiled at him and explained that I owed RMB 200 to the Telecommunications Bureau and refused to pay them the RMB 900 they were demanding.

He asked how it was that I was so handsome and still owed other people and why I was smiling. Afterwards, he said, "I dislike you. Fellows, beat him. Beat him hard!"

At once, more than twenty prisoners in the room started to beat me. I felt that my entire torso was nearly broken. After they beat me, they poured cold water on me. I could hardly tolerate such humiliation and knelt down to beg the man in charge to set me free.

The head threatened me, "Do not smile again; otherwise, I will beat you one more time. Make a face for us now."

I could only follow his order.

At that moment, I swore that if I were to walk out of there someday, I would definitely accuse all of the world in front of God.

The thing I do today is to practise the promise I'd made in jail—to accuse all the world. I titled my book *Battle of the New Era* and added the subtitle *A Diary Written to God, Accusing All the World*.

My wife saved me from jail on the second day. I am really grateful to my now ex-wife, and I love her very much. She married me after I'd moved down in the world, and she saved me from jail in an emergency.

Such emotion cannot be measured by money. My ex-wife is the person who treats me best and loves me the most in the world, like my grandmother did when she was alive.

In 2004, I and my wife bought our public rental house and made it our private property. My grandmother lived in Anhui at that time. After learning the news, she asked me to return to Anhui and refused to add the name of my wife to the property ownership certificate. My grandmother insisted on adding my name and her own name to the certificate instead. Therefore, she asked that I go back home to see the house property notary. The notary declared that the house was my personal property irrespective of my wife.

When I returned to Shanghai, I discussed this matter with my wife. Although she was very unhappy, she complied. We went to the notary office to apply for the property notary.

The notary later played a decisive and crucial role in the publication of *Battle of the New Era*.

The house was not available to my wife, and our copier repair business was doing worse as the market changed. We could no longer make money. We had to find a new business. We have set up several businesses, but all of them had failed.

These two reasons led to the intensification of my conflict with my wife, and finally I had to divorce under the pressure of her family.

Although we divorced, my personal relationship with my ex-wife is still good. We continue to live together, and she suggests that we have a baby.

After our marriage, when my wife thought about having children, I refused for various reasons. There was always a voice telling me that if

I had a baby, I wouldn't be able to do what God had told me to do and I wouldn't be able to finish the *Battle of the New Era*. If I had children, I would have no time or energy to write or study. Time and energy should be spent on the child. And the thing I hate most is the sound of a baby crying.

Once I hear the cry of a child, my head explodes. Nothing can be done about this. Children are demons to me. So I'm most afraid of having a baby.

So during the half-year I lived with my wife, I refused to have a child because I had some minor problems. She and I eventually bid farewell to each other in tears.

All I had to do was ask my wife to stay and say that my house would be half hers, and then she would have stayed. But God told me that this house could not be given to my wife because it would be needed to finish *Battle of the New Era*. So I didn't ask my wife to stay. So to speak, I turned her away.

Another reason I left my wife had to do with energy. When I get close to, within a certain distance of, people, especially women, I experience some bad effects.

I have lived with my ex-wife for three years, and we have been together every day. We hold hands when we go out, and we hug when we go to bed. We had a great relationship. Physically I liked my ex-wife very much.

But I never told anyone that mentally, I am like a steak in a pan every day. I'd been cooking this steak for three years since I'd met my ex-wife.

It is not just my ex-wife, but all people, especially women. As soon as you get close to me, I become greatly disturbed. I lose energy, and I become very uncomfortable.

I like beautiful women very much, but I am also very afraid of them. Their bad influence on me makes me very angry.

So if you have anything to tell me, you can tell me. If you have finished what you want to say, please leave now. Don't try to get close to me.

Leaving my wife was a relief to me. I will never go back to my ex-wife. But I am very grateful to her. I love her very much.

Sometimes when I think of my ex-wife, I cry.

Why did God let me do such a difficult thing? My ex-wife loves me so much. What reason did I have for abandoning her?

God told me that if I didn't leave her, that if I didn't write the *Battle of the New Era*, a great many people all over the world would die. This was nothing compared to one person's happiness and gain. So I had no choice.

I told my wife when we were separating, "God sent you to help me through this difficult time. Now that your mission is complete, you can go." She was very unhappy, though she was understanding.

I promised my ex-wife that if I ever got rich, I would repay her.

So if any of you ever meet my ex-wife, please help her and her family. I promised her that I would continue to love her, and I appreciate her.

ADVICE OFFERED TO REFORM STATE-OWNED ENTERPRISES

I am devoted to business for certain reasons. I attempt to find out which of Marx's doctrines, and whether or not his theories about capitalism, are accurate. I test these ideas with my views and with practise, according to my cognition level.

I am a good man, and I plan to find out if a good man will be well rewarded in doing business.

In April 2004, when the new Chinese national leader came to power, there was a test, the Tieben Event. I came up with an inspiration all of a sudden as if being compelled by God. The questions I had been pondering all seemed to have been answered, so I had to write down the inspiration immediately.

I have written five articles on the reform of state-owned enterprises in China. The major economists in China at the time appealed to sell out all the state-owned enterprises, while my proposal to reform state-owned enterprises by separating the right to management from ownership is exactly the opposite in nature. I proposed to strengthen the management of the Central Committee of the Communist Party of China (CPC) as relating to the ownership of state-owned enterprises and to completely liberalize the management right of state-owned enterprises.

I broadly disbursed the five articles by sending letters and emails to each national committee and government authority which was attached with great importance to the Central Committee of the CPC.

Someone from Central Party School of the Communist Party of China invited me to post my articles in the school forum.

A few days later, it was displayed in the headline of the website State-Owned Assets Supervision and Administration Commission of the State Council that the reform directive of state-owned enterprises was to separate the right of management and ownership instead of selling out. I argued that the government should stop the privatization reform of state-owned enterprises.

At the very moment that state-owned enterprises and the ruling foundation of the CPC were to be thoroughly destroyed, I offered national-scale advice to China which instantly reversed the situation for the state-owned enterprises that were about to be sold out, maintained the ruling foundation of the CPC, and strengthened the CPC's comprehensive and scientific control over state-owned enterprises.

Furthermore, the reform directive of state-owned enterprises to separate the right of management and ownership has survived up to today and has become the most basic condition of, and the foundation for, Chinese political stability, highly efficient economic development, and scientific national governance.

Without my proposal to separate the right of management and ownership of state-owned enterprises, China would have been in chaos for a long time, similar to or even worse than the chaos the Soviet Union experienced after dissolution.

The national operation model I proposed to the Chinese government in 2004 is exactly the national operation model that can be promoted worldwide. I hope that the whole world can refer to this Chinese model and execute it.

This model is named as the China model. I proposed the design concept of the China model. In other words, I was the behind-the-scenes chief designer.

In addition, I have witnessed China operating according to this model for dozens of years, so I know all the secrets of this model. Today, I am here to divulge the original code of this model to the whole world. You can modify the code in accordance with your real-life situations and to fit your national development demands.

I had been thinking of why there was such a huge conflict between students, the CPC, and the government in the time period of the Tiananmen Square event. Which of these parties was right? Now I can tell you my answer.

The contradiction between the student movement and the Communist Party boils down to the contradiction between capitalism and communism, that is, between democratic freedom and social governance.

The student movement accentuates democratic freedom and completely ignores social governance.

Certainly, it is wrong that sometimes the Communist Party overemphasizes social governance and social order while totally overlooking democratic freedom.

For a society that runs on sound scientific governance, democratic freedom and social governance are complementary rather than contradictory.

Social governance, social order, and social justice are the pillars of a country and a society, and they make up the skeleton of the society and the framework of the basic structure. Democratic freedom is the body, muscles, blood, fat, and internal organs of a society.

Therefore, it cannot be called wrong that the student movement expressed public opinion in the Tiananmen Square event, but the movement should have been temperate and should have shown respect to social governance and government authority. That is to say, expressing the public opinion should not have gone any further than necessary. A timely retreat would have prevented the subsequent tragedy.

The Tiananmen Square event evolved to the point where it went beyond expressing public opinion to expression the hope of coercing or even overthrowing the government.

Some of the protesters burned soldiers alive, which was enough to evidence the illegality of their actions.

As a result, the government took some necessary measures.

To realize social governance, social fairness and justice, and scientific management of a society entails untold money, because fairness and justice cannot be manipulated by people, and fairness and justice cannot be measured by money, nor can they be bought and distorted by money.

State-owned capital plays a decisive role in ensuring fairness and justice, realizing the scientific management of society, giving play to the supporting function of social operation.

My theory is to use the wealth created by God to realize the law of God, to realize the fairness and justice of a society, and to realize the scientific management of society.

In my theory, some monopolistic enterprises and resource-based enterprises, as well as public ownership of land, provide sufficient funds for the scientific social management of government, so that the government is able to operate independently and is no longer subject to capitalists and taxpayers.

Besides, the government must operate independently in accordance with the principles of fairness, justice, and scientific management.

Private ownership and democracy is the effective complement to the government. Both need to develop soundly and vigorously.

Fairness and justice at the national level can truly protect the private property of citizens.

The government takes advantage of a large amount of state-owned capital to guide and adjust the economy running towards scientific growth. This is also the benefit of the government framework for the private economy. The two complement each other.

The Practical Application of Marx's Theory of Exploitation

Marx believes that public ownership is superior to private ownership because public ownership eliminates exploitation.

After practising as a boss for many years, I have figured this out. This assertion of Marx cannot be deemed completely wrong, nor can it be seen as being completely correct. It holds water under certain conditions:

1) Broadly defined exploitation and narrowly defined exploitation

Any act of possessing surplus value is called exploitation. This is what is known as broadly defined exploitation.

In narrowly defined exploitation, labourers are paid a wage recognized by both parties in the process of hiring labour, which is not called exploitation. Forced labour, in which the labourer does not recognize the labour price, is narrowly defined exploitation, for example sex slaves or slavery.

2) Relative and absolute exploitation

Absolute exploitation, similar to narrowly defined exploitation, refers to exploitation in the form of forced labour. If there is an agreement in advance and the boss pays wages as the labour contract stipulates, then it is not forced labour.

An example of relative exploitation is to be found in two companies that sell the same product, employ the same workers, and produce the same products and surplus value, but one is a state-owned enterprise and the other is a private enterprise.

The owner of the private enterprise takes the surplus value of the company, several billion yuan, to pay dividends to shareholders and himself. This is a legal act because the surplus value of the private sector is owned by the shareholders.

When the same behaviour occurs in state-owned enterprises, for example the employers of state-owned enterprises distribute billions to themselves and senior executives without the state's permission, this is a corrupt act. Because state-owned enterprises are owned by the state and the money earned by state-owned enterprises also belongs to the state (i.e. it is state-owned capital), the bosses of state-owned enterprises have no right to give themselves bonuses or benefits.

The profit of state-owned enterprises is used by the state for social governance and operation. The more money a state-owned enterprise makes, the greater the interests of the people are. This is a boon for the people of the whole society.

The profits of a private company are owned by its owners and shareholders. No matter how much money a private company makes, it has nothing to do with the national. No other national can enjoy any benefit from the profitability of the private sector. This situation only widens the gap between the rich and the poor.

Compared to developing state-owned enterprises, developing private enterprises bring far fewer benefits to the public. Therefore we say that private enterprises carry out relative exploitation.

From the perspective of relative exploitation, the scientific development of state-owned enterprises is in the best interests of the people. But the vast majority of people do not understand it. This is an expression of human ignorance. It is the main point of my book, *Battle of the New Era*.

The foregoing represent my main views on China's state-owned enterprise reform since 2004. My theoretical contributions have been recognized by the government and have been followed since I made the proposal.

In 2004, I stopped the sale of six hundred billion New Taiwan dollars' worth of US arms to Taiwan. A world war was prevented.

In October 2004, I was informed that Taiwan planned to spend six hundred billion New Taiwanese dollars to buy arms from the United States. If such a plan were implemented, considering China's policy towards Taiwan, it would inevitably have led to a war across the strait, and the United States would certainly have participated in the war. With the strength of China at that time, it was impossible to win a war against the United States. A direct confrontation with the nuclear power would have catastrophic and devastating to the while world.

By God's grace, I immediately wrote an article titled "Let's Make Up" and emailed it to hundreds of thousands of people in Taiwan. Back then the network did not have a filtering system for email. After I sent that email, the people instantly received it.

My article exerted a huge amount influence on the Taiwanese people. Dramatically, the arms purchase was cancelled. Moreover, representatives of the Kuomintang came to the mainland for a friendly visit. The president of Taiwan at the time, Chen Shui-bian, was sent to prison and has not been released yet. The Kuomintang won the next election, and Ma Ying-jeou came to power.

This was the result of sending an email at the most critical moment for humankind. I stopped the war and saved all your lives. You can find the article "Let's Make Up" in *Battle of the New Era, Book 2.*

MY GRANDMA PASSED AWAY IN 2005

Shortly after I divorced my wife, my grandma returned to Shanghai because of illness. Accompanying my grandma were my two aunts. They said that Grandma had inflammation and needed to be operated on. They asked me to sell my house so that Grandma could afford to get medical treatment.

My business had failed at the time. I didn't have a job then, and my physical condition was not good. Moreover, I had given all the money my wife and I had earned during the course of our marriage to my ex-wife.

When I divorced my wife, we split our property. After we'd done the calculations, it became clear that she had helped me pay some debts and buy a house. Moreover, in the previous few years, her parents had been helping us do business wholeheartedly. So it was reasonable to give them some of the money left in our bank account.

I was penniless at the time my grandma was ill, and I had nothing other than the house, the property under my name, to rely on. If I were to sell the house, I would have nothing. So I was unwilling to sell the house.

After a few weeks, we learned that Grandma's inflammation turned out to be advanced cancer. The doctor suggested that my grandmother should not have any operation since she was already ninety-seven years old.

Then all my grandmother's children came to Shanghai to say goodbye to my grandma. My relatives were very dissatisfied that I had gotten the house. But I would not agree to sell the house, and they could not do anything.

My grandma was the person who loved me the most in the world. When all of the family members disapproved of me, she still stood by my side, even at the cost of her life. This is what a relative of mine told me later.

I was penniless when my grandma was dying. I couldn't do nothing but watch her decline day by day.

Those who are nearest to me and love me the most were hurt by me the deepest.

The only thing I could do was to lie next to my grandma for a while. This was what little comfort I could offer.

In a few days, my grandma passed away.

When I rushed back to see her body, I found that her eyes remained open, and no one could make her eyes stay closed. I looked at her and felt that she had not left. So I said to the people in the room, "You all go out. I have something to say to my grandma alone."

Holding my grandmother's hand, I said to her, "Grandma, God has sent me on a mission. Everything I've done is not for myself. I am for all. If you see God, he will tell you all this. Just go well."

I felt that my grandmother listened to what I had said and really left. I covered her eyes gently, at which time her eyes closed.

ORGANIZING DRAFTS INTO ARTICLES FROM 2005 TO 2007

After my grandma's funeral, my relatives left, leaving me alone in the empty house.

I rented out the house and then rented a smaller house elsewhere, using the difference in rents as my living allowance. I discussed national events with various people on the Internet. While having intense debates with various types of netizens, I organized my speeches into articles.

Since 2007, the Chinese government has strictly controlled online speech. Any article that did not meet their criteria was deleted, and many forums were closed. Most of my articles were deleted from the Internet. Luckily, I had organized them, and most of my articles were stored on my computer.

I didn't think there was anything worth discussing on the Internet, so I started looking for a job.

BECOMING IRON-WILLED THROUGH REPEATED ROUGH EXPERIENCES AT AN INSURANCE COMPANY

In the second half of 2007, I was employed by a state-owned insurance company.

At that time, insurance companies offered the darkest and most terrible job prospects. There was no basic salary, no pension, no medical insurance, and no social security for the salesmen, who had only marketing tasks to complete.

Of course, there are also high-income people in insurance companies. As long as the right methods are applied, one can earn some money. My teacher was a very good salesperson. I followed my teacher to start working as a salesman. It took me six years to be appointed as a sales manager. I had led a team of seventy people at most.

We had a variety of trainings every week, every month, and every year, mainly on negotiation skills, product learning, and team management.

I joined the insurance company mainly because it offered a most challenging profession that allowed me to contact the greatest number of people. I needed to reach out to a wide variety of people to understand this society. I needed to negotiate with a wide variety of people to develop my own negotiating skills and an ability to communicate with others. Meanwhile, I also exercised my ability to speak publicly.

These were all things I wanted to learn. I deliberately chose to exercise my abilities in an extremely challenging environment that was both rough and complex.

Looking back, I see that I had not been able to make ends meet previously. It was only when I worked in the insurance company that I made a little money. I was very grateful to my teacher in the company.

I had learned the importance of respecting the teacher in the insurance company. Although I had a little friction with my teacher, I did everything I could to save face with her. Du Yuesheng, modern China's former number one Shanghai gangster, once said that life's three elements are (1) respectful feelings, (2) respect in public, and (3) face-saving. I gave them all to my teacher.

So I maintained an excellent private relationship with my teacher, who had helped me out of many difficulties.

In the two years I served as a manager, I gave forty thousand yuan back to my aunt and also paid off the debts I owed to several friends.

God told me that I would never again in this lifetime owe anyone money. Only others would owe me.

I BUILT MY PERSONAL WEBSITE AND PROMOTED IT ALL OVER THE WORLD IN 2013

I worked as a manager of the insurance company in 2012, and it was a special year. It was allegedly the end of the world. That year was very strange. I felt that someone was supervising me during that period.

However, I was very busy every day, leading my team to sell insurance products. I didn't do anything weird, so there was nothing about me to be monitored.

In July 2013, I opened my own personal website, organized all my articles and uploaded them, and promoted the website to the world.

Although I didn't know who had viewed my website, I felt that it began to have an international influence. What I wrote on the website would be known to important people around the world.

I kept writing my diary on my website. I also wrote my thoughts and made comments about some important events around the world on the website. I would tell God about these things, and people from all over the world would give me positive responses.

THE ISLAMIC STATE MADLY KILLED PEOPLE, AND I STOOD UP FOR JUSTICE

On August 20, 2014, when I learned about the atrocities of the Islamic State on television, I was furious. I wrote an article essentially yelling at the Islamic State.

The next day I saw President Obama saying on TV, "God does not support the Islamic State, and their ideology is bankrupt."

For the first time, I clearly felt God's response to me. And it was so fast and so determined that I felt God was very close to me.

As you can see from later developments, the United States–led countries established an alliance against the Islamic State and began to bomb them. After that, the Islamic State embarked on the road to destruction. They have basically disappeared now.

From that point on, I wrote intensively against Islamic extremism and criticized the allies of Islamic extremist forces in Western countries. My articles were mainly comments on Islam and my take on what happened in Western countries.

Not only did I upload the articles I wrote to my website, but also, when something critical happened in the world, I translated my articles into English and Arabic to spread them widely on the network.

I found that whenever I distributed these articles, the relevant countries would respond accordingly and make changes. The political situation in the world would change in turn, and positive changes would take place in the direction I wanted.

The purpose of spreading my articles is to convince people to stop supporting the devil and doing the wrong things. I hope to correct people's wrong thinking and practices. We should concentrate on fighting against the devil if we want to save the world.

In fact, I did this myself. God helped me. God supported me.

The articles I wrote appear in edited form in *Battle of the New Era*, and each article appears under a general subhead that indicates the month and year in which it was written. You can verify everything I have said and see how God supported my points of view by looking at the time of writing, my ideas, and the subsequent dramatic changes in the world's political situation.

- After August 2014, my comments were mainly related to Islam and Western countries.
- I mainly commented on and paid attention to the war in Syria. I supported Syrian government forces when they began to retreat

and were about to perish. Now they have regained control of the situation.

- I proposed that Yemen needed to start a war to fight against extreme Islam. It declared war immediately.
- I proposed that China help Syria. As a result, Russia immediately sent troops to Syria.
- I proposed that Trump should be elected president of the United States.
- I proposed that Iran and North Korea should not have nuclear weapons. Then Iran signed a nuclear agreement.
- I criticized North Korea and asked China to draw a line in the sand with North Korea. I wrote several articles about North Korea.
- I criticized Turkey for helping Islamic extremists.
- I proposed to defend the Kurds against Islamic extremists.
- I proposed that Saudi Arabia return to moderate Islam.

IN 2015, I SOLD MY HOUSE AND PUBLISHED BATTLE OF THE NEW ERA

In the second half of 2015, I sold the house that my grandma had left me. When I got the money, I first paid a large sum I owed to a friend, including interest. Then I began to prepare for the publication of *Battle of the New Era*. I started to contact publishing houses in 2016. The publishers said that my book was politically sensitive in nature and that these kinds of books were not allowed to be published in China. They said that my book could only be published overseas.

I found an overseas agent and asked him to help me publish this book abroad. So I started to translate all my articles into English, and I proofread the articles. I spent a lot of money on having the articles translated and publishing the book and a long time proofreading my articles. Finally, *Battle of the New Era* was published in November 2016.

I asked my agent to help me advertise and promote the book, but he said that he was very busy and refused my request.

When I published *Battle of the New Era* the first time, I saw it for sale on Amazon. I was very happy. I thought that people would buy my book, but no one made a purchase.

In June 2017, I decided to personally contact the publishers, advertise myself, and republish my book. I added a lot of new articles to the updated version.

I spent almost all my money and suffered many setbacks in my work. I just want to meet everyone today and provide them with the opportunity to know me and my book.

I have not done anything else in this life apart from writing this book. I am completing the task that God has given to me. I hope you enjoy my book.

I believe that my book can bring wealth, happiness, and the love of God to all who read it.

PART II

THE AUTHOR ANSWERS QUESTIONS FROM REPORTERS

George Walker

QUESTIONS RAISED BY THE FIRST REPORTER

October 2018

WHAT DO YOU HAVE TO SAY ABOUT YOUR BOOK?

On the topic of my religious faith, I have this to say:

After I arrived in the Philippines, a friend asked me a very interesting question: "What is your religious faith?"

I said, "I have no religious faith, or I believe in all religions." But to say it more exactly, I believe in all religions. That states it in clear words. I believe in one God.

The principle is simple. All religions agree that God created the world. And we all know that all of us are living on earth; we are living in this world. We are living in the same space and time, so the space and time above this earth was created by one God.

We are from different nations, different races, and different cultures, as well as different religions. However, in reality, all religions believe in the same God.

In my opinion, Islam, Christianity, Buddhism, and Taoism in China, the mainstream and acknowledged religions, believe in the same God.

Also, I believe that communism and capitalism are enlightened ideas that have come to humankind from our God. It is God's will that some countries and some people believe in capitalism and that some countries and some people believe in communism.

Islam, Christianity, Buddhism, Taoism, communism, and capitalism are very useful; they are the expression of great truth to the human race. And I believe that something that can be called the great truth can't be created by any individual but only by our God.

No individual, no matter how clever he or she is, can create any part of the great truth and convince people all around the world of it. This is impossible. Only God can create the great truth.

This book talks about the great truth.

I believe everybody knows the story of 2012 being the end of the world. Why did this story appear?

As the great truth has been taught by our God, with the great truth including the tenets of Islam, Christianity, Buddhism, and Taoism, it has been passed down from generation to generation for two thousand to three thousand years. All supernatural power from these religions has disappeared.

At the beginning of any of these religions, the religion could coordinate social relations. However, after thousands of years, the supernatural power has now disappeared.

So 2012 was thought to be the end of the world, as the religions created by God could not play their roles anymore. That's why it was called the end of the world.

At present we are standing in the end time of religion, the time when the supernatural power of religion will disappear.

So the world we are standing in now is full of confusion and disasters.

Why is it that these disasters have appeared just as the supernatural power of religions has disappeared?

God gave me a mission to share with other people my wish that everyone on earth will build a new faith and come to a new consensus, the likes of which is written about in my book.

If you were to ask me what faith I am trying to get you to accept, I would say that I have not created any faith; I just have settled all faiths that God has expressed to us.

The *Battle of the New Era* series is around one thousand pages in length. In this book, I have criticized all countries of the world, everything that exists, and every aspect of every religion that I do not think is good.

I always criticize people, but I rarely praise people.

However, it's strange that I have praised the Philippine president Mr Duterte in my diary. And I have reserved my best comments for President Duterte. I say that he is Saint Seiya delivered by God to save us.

Who is Saint Seiya? He is the soldier of God, the warrior protecting God, maintaining fairness and justice.

God delivered President Duterte to help the Philippine people root out evil.

A few days ago, I stayed in Manila for a few hours. I took a taxi and circled around to view the living conditions of people in Manila. I spent three hours viewing Manila. I went to the governmental hall of Manila, Chinatown, the largest hotel, and the most crowded shopping mall, and so on.

When I was in the taxicab, I asked the driver, "Do you think the city you are living in is safe?"

The driver answered me very quickly: "Since Duterte became our president, Manila has become the world's safest city." He said he likes President Duterte very much.

The driver didn't know who I was. He did not know that I would give a speech on the radio that day. He thought that I was just an ordinary Chinese tourist, so I believe what he said is the expression of the true will of the people.

In my writings, I rarely praise others. I have praised President Duterte and Donald John Trump.

Before Trump was selected as the president I have since praised, I wished he would be the president, and I wrote many articles to that effect. During Trump's presidential campaign and before he was president, I wrote many articles praising him.

One of my articles was selected and used by Trump's son. For example, in my book you will read an article on the topic of the toxic apple. That term was altered by the younger Trump to read "toxic rainbow". The Rainbow Hall prosecuted the younger Trump.

The basic argument and content of Trump's son's article is the same as my article. If you are interested in this, please find this article in this book to verify what I have said.

I also have praised Bashar al-Assad, president of Syria. In his most difficult time, when everybody thought he would fail, I supported him and praised him, believing he would succeed.

Assad represents secular society, whereas those who oppose him in the war represent Islamic extremism. I believe that Islamic extremism is evil, so I insisted on supporting Assad.

I think the most outstanding example of God supporting me is that I forced North Korea to give up on the use of force and remain at peace with South Korea. Why would Donald Trump be such a strong influence on North Korea? Why would the Chinese government give up on protecting North Korea? Why would Russia give up on protecting North Korea?

Do you not feel there is something strange about this?

Why would everyone in the world be against North Korea, with no country daring to help North Korea? Because I asked them to do this.

On my website and in my book, I published a lot of articles about North Korea. My influence was one hundred times stronger than Trump's.

I named North Korea as an evil country, saying that if North Korea refused to capitulate, then God would destroy the country completely.

So all countries of the world were quiet. No country dared to help North Korea anymore. North Korea was lonely without any help, so they capitulated. They were forced to concede because of my pressure.

Of course, if North Koreans change their minds and switch to the right side, God will forgive them. God will also love North Korea and Kim Jong-un.

I write my opinions about the world in my diary so as to report to God.

As a result, God reads my diary and gives me affirmative answers.

Basically, all that I have written in my diary has come true. I think it is very strange. Why does God believe in me to such a great degree?

For example, I supported the Assad regime when it was at a low. The consequence was that the regime stabilized. It is not an effective thing to oppose Assad's regime no matter how many people are against it. Because God supports me and God believes in me, God will help the Assad regime.

All I wrote in the diary will be approved by God.

Each of my diary entries is accompanied by the date of writing. You can look in my book or on my website, find what was happening in the world at the time, read what is written in my diary, and see the changes that took place in the world after my writing.

How does God support me? You can verify that he does by looking in my book or on my website.

I think there are too many people who love to tell tall tales or speak nonsense. And Westerners like to do experiments to verify something.

I welcome you to verify that what I am saying is true. You can look at each of my diary entries to determine whether my predictions came true and find what things were like before and after what I'd said would happen happened if you wish to discover God's attitude towards me.

You may think that one or two coincidences don't prove anything, but if a coincidence occurs every time, should it not be determined that God is with me?

God definitely and totally believes in me and cooperates with me.

I don't dare to say that I'm the envoy of the God, because then someone will ask to see my license. They will say, "Show me the license that God has issued to you." Which I can't do, obviously. I don't know whether God gives me a license or not. Why does he choose me to do such things?

What I can do is only suggest that you do your experiments to prove my words true. Look at the changes in the world after my writing. All are proven and judged by scientific logic, right?

The result you get from your scientific experiments, whether it be that God supports me or not, is your scientific conclusion. It's not my nonsense, and I don't need to show you a license from God.

WHY DID YOU PUBLISH IT?

I had no choice. God guided me.

WHEN YOU WERE STILL WRITING THE MANUSCRIPT, HAD YOU EVER THOUGHT NOT TO PUBLISH THE BOOK?

Since my junior high school years, I have found that my ideas are different from others. In my mind, I hear someone always talking to me, telling me I need to write a book and distribute it across the world.

When something happens to me, I will not stop thinking about it until I find the answers. For instance, the Chinese political event that happened in 1989 was a very serious political conflict. How were the Chinese Communist Party representing the benefits of ordinary people and the students representing democratic revolution compatible?

When I have some thoughts, I write them down. What I think is not only about the political conflict; it is also about everything that has happened in human history that has been thought, written down, and studied.

I clear up all these events through the articles in my book.

In other words, it has taken my whole life to write this book, and the book can be widely distributed. This has always been my life's dream.

WHY DO YOU WANT TO SPREAD THE WORD OR THE MESSAGE?

I think God dispatched me to save everyone on earth. I always work for God and save the world, just nobody knows it. I work secretly.

I just want to tell you today that I have succeeded. What I want to do today is to announce to the world how I work, how I save the world. I hope you will prove that what I say is true by studying my book, my website, and my diary.

DID SOMEONE HELP YOU TO FINISH THE BOOK?

Every word in this book was written by me and then translated by a translation company. This book has magical power. No one dares read it, never mind write it.

This series of books has over three hundred articles, and the translation required about one hundred translators. One person refused to translate my articles, and someone even called the police after reading my book.

When I was writing this book, I prayed that no terrorists would find me.

If someone wants to kill me because of this book, just come; I don't mind. Because of all the people and all the things that have let me down, and because of everyone who doesn't like me, I can leave the world at any time. I don't mind.

WHY ARE YOU CONCERNED WITH THE PEOPLE?

I think that if I don't do this, nobody will do this. If I don't say something, then nobody will say anything. If I didn't do these things, the world would be ruined.

Actually, I have prevented many wars and saved the lives of everyone on earth. I prevented an attack on China, a war in Korea, and a war in the Middle East.

IF YOU END UP HAVING ONE HUNDRED COPIES OF YOUR BOOK PRINTED, HOW WILL YOU USE THEM?

I hope I can send one copy each to one hundred libraries so that more people can read it.

AS AUTHOR OF THIS BOOK, WHAT MADE YOU DECIDE TO PROMOTE THE BOOK IN THE PHILIPPINES?

I always try to spread word of the book to the whole world. I published this book three times, and I spent a lot of money advertising it. But it has all been for naught. Several months ago, someone called me to advertise this book in the Philippines and South East Asia, so I came to the Philippines.

I know people accept a concept, a book, an author, or an artist, although sometimes it takes a long time for them to do so. A particular artist may have a poor life, but decades after his death, he becomes accepted by the world. I don't mind being such an artist. If I die poor in the street, I won't mind. I will never give up my dream.

I have been very lucky to meet all of you after having taken this chance. The Filipinos accepted me first. I like the Philippines. Thank you very much.

George Walker

QUESTIONS RAISED BY THE SECOND REPORTER

October 2018

What are the things that you like about Donald Trump?

Almost all of Trump's ideas came from my website, such as his ideas about immigrants, extremist Islam, white supremacy, nationalism, North Korea, and fake news. Although I have never seen Trump, he is like my best student. So I like him. During his campaign, I wrote a lot of articles to support him. In my diary, I called for an influence on American voters to help the Trump campaign. I just thought it was fun to talk about it casually. But I didn't expect it to be realized. God completely cooperated with me. Even I was surprised.

Do you consider the Syrian war to be a mini world war? If yes, why? If no, please give us your opinion about it.

The point that the Syrian war is a small world war is not my point of view but the view of Chinese netizens. Since August 2014, every day I have collected various data from the Internet on Syria, Iraq, the Middle East as a whole, Islam, Iran, Turkey, Qatar, Saudi Arabia, Yemen, East Turkestan, Hezbollah, Israel, and other countries. I know nothing about the Middle East before, but I became an expert a few months later. I gradually figured out the primary causes of the complex situation in the Middle East.

Qatar and Saudi Arabia had asked to construct an oil pipeline with direct access to the Mediterranean Sea in Syria. But the Syrian president refused their request. Only Iran's oil pipeline is allowed to pass through Syrian territory. So the two richest countries in the Middle East, Saudi Arabia and Qatar, have to rely on ISIS and other terrorist organizations, and the power of Islamic extremist forces, to overthrow the Assad regime. They have poured money into terrorist organizations and paid the terrorists' monthly wages.

Turkey, a country neighbouring Syria, has the job of recruiting terrorists, training terrorists, and delivering large quantities of weapons to Syria. East Turkestan terrorists in China are recruited, trained, transported, and replenished by Turkey. They are still active in Idlib, Syria. You can interview them if you are not afraid of death.

The Western countries are the whore spoken of in the book of Revelation. Taking money from Saudi Arabia and Qatar, the politicians of Western countries completely abandon fairness and justice, providing political protection and military weapons for terrorists. The purpose is to help Saudi Arabia and Qatar overthrow Syrian president Bashar al-Assad. In the final analysis, it is for the benefit of money and oil.

The West still claims to have overthrown Assad. I asked the Chinese government to send troops to Syria to help the Assad regime. Instead of doing so, the Chinese government bought a lot of oil and gas from Russia and provided a lot of money to Russia. Russia helped Assad. And the Chinese government has supported Syrian government forces at the UN political level.

All the forces in the world have competed in Syria. The United States also directly attacked the Syrian government forces. They used white helmets to create fake news and slander Syrian government forces, using chemical weapons to directly attack the Syrian government. But it is only a show, and it cannot change the direction of the situation in Syria.

The Syrian government forces were retreating step by step and were about to die when I first paid attention to them. After I intervened, the Syrian government gained full control over the entire territory of Syria.

I recognize that the situation in Syria has been decided basically. I will no longer care about Syria. It can generally be said that all the mainstream countries of the world are involved in the Syrian war. They have directly and indirectly participated in the Syrian war, so it is called a small world war.

In order to contain the forces of Saudi Arabia, Qatar, and the Middle East and disperse their strength, attention, and financial resources, I wrote an article in support of the Houthi rebels in Yemen to launch an armed conflict. As a result, within a few days after I'd written the article, Yemen immediately broke out in war, a war that has not yet ended This is another example of God's support for me.

Who is behind the Syrian war?

Saudi Arabia, Qatar, Turkey, the United States, Great Britain, France, Germany, and Israel together all support ISIS and other terrorist organizations and Islamic extremist groups in the attempt to overthrow Assad.

Russia, Iran, Hezbollah, China, and I are all for Assad, for justice, and for secular, moderate, and inclusive Islam. Of course, God is on our side because God trusts me and supports me.

Who do you think will win the Syrian war?

Assad.

What should we do to help the situation in Syria?

We need to oppose the white helmet and stop them from creating fake news. We must refuse to be deceived by Western propaganda machines. We should support moderate Islam and oppose extreme Islam.

What other things do you like about Donald Trump?

President Obama supports extreme Islam, and the best thing Trump does is to oppose extreme Islam.

To support Trump in stopping terrorism is to help God fight evil.

This is the best thing Trump has ever done. I like people who do things for God. Trump was sent by God to help him fight against evil terrorists.

Do you consider Trump to be the best president of the United States so far? If yes, why? If no, who was the best president of the USA?

There have been many great presidents of the United States who have done different things for the United States at different times, and everything was important according to the circumstances of the respective presidencies. Because of the different conditions and environments, any comparison is irrelevant. And I really don't know exactly what every US president has done, so I can't comment.

What do you have to say about the people who dislike and disrespect Trump?

I have a bad reputation on the Internet, and I often seriously argue with others about certain matters. Sometimes I even use the most vulgar words. Many netizens can't bear my behaviour and leave the discussion. Of course, their hearts were badly hurt.

Trump's words have been gentle enough; he is a good boy compared to me.

If I curse someone, it will be one hundred times more severe than if Trump does so. Of course, one hundred times more people dislike me. But I don't care.

What are your reasons for wanting to help the people of this world?

I don't know why I came to this world. If I could make a choice, I would not come here to do so many things.

However, I have come to this world. I would certainly start well and end well because life is short. Maybe I will die after a while. I wish that during my lifetime I could do very meaningful and valuable things for the world. And what I do is irreplaceable. Each of us is striving for life every day; no one cares what happens in the world. I just do something that no one has ever done. I don't think how smart or great I am. I only know that you don't do what I do; I am the only one who does. I just do the thing that I think is the most valuable thing I could do with my life. The value is immeasurable. Because certain things would never be done if I didn't do them. Some ideas would never be expressed if I didn't speak them out.

You said that if people read your book, they will get rich. Why would the readers get rich?

China's national management model was established according to my ideas. I hope to establish a model and perform an experiment in China to verify my theory.

Facts have proved that my theory is successful. China is now widely recognized by the whole world for its social stability and the affluence of its population. I hope that after reading my book, you in the Philippines will manage your country in accordance with the Chinese model and implement the national management system I have established, so you can realize the same level of social stability and affluence as China and gradually realize the fairness and justice in such a system.

My book describes in detail how to establish the Chinese model and the ideal national management system as I have imagined them.

There are some problems with China's current situation because the Chinese government has partially adopted my suggestions but rejected some of my proposals.

The ruling class accepts what benefits them without hesitation, just as the saying, "An aircraft carrier can turn 180 degrees on a dollar coin." But suggestions that are disadvantageous, restraining, or punitive to the ruling class are completely ignored. That's the ugly truth.

Nevertheless, China is still the most successful country in the world when it comes to having achieved national governance.

I hope you can learn from my national management system and management model so that you, along with everyone else in the world, can get rich.

Do you think each country will need your book? Why?

Without a doubt. Because all countries of the world have serious domestic problems, everyone in every country can find solutions and suggestions in my book. Moreover, the solutions and suggestions are effective. So every country and everyone needs my book.

You said that God gave you this mission to spread your story. Do you think you can complete this mission? To what extent can you complete your mission?

God's mission as given to me is that I transmit my ideas to those in trouble, to those needing my help, and to those needing my advice.

Since 2004, I have been providing advice and wisdom to governments and politicians of all countries, so as to help them solve problems, solve crises, save the world, and prevent the world from being destroyed from human actions and recklessness.

I have written this book and publicized it on a wide scale because I have completed the mission. I have helped all countries and all politicians. I have given them the most intelligent advice. Most of them have adopted my suggestions, and I have solved the most serious crisis in the world

I am here today to tell all the people of the world what I have done rather than having only a few politicians know what I did.

I hope all the people of the world can follow my idea. I hope to make suggestions to everyone on earth rather than just limiting my advice to a few politicians.

I hope to help all the people of the world and not just a few politicians.

Earlier, you told me that you like President Duterte. What do you have to say about the killings that are happening in the Philippines?

There would be no shootings in the Philippines if there were no drugs. God hates drugs, and the war against drug dealers is a war between God and the devil.

If drugs do not disappear, the devil will not disappear, and the war will not stop. Of course, the shooting will not stop because some of you are still helping the devil and abandoning God.

QUESTIONS RAISED BY THE THIRD REPORTER

October 2018

What things do you want to see happen in the world over the next five years?

I hope that my book will be promoted and spread all over the world. Since I don't know how fast the book will be distributed, I find it hard to imagine what will happen in five years.

I hope that this book will have made its way all over the world in five years. Then people all over the world will understand what I really want to express in this book so they can accept my suggestions and set up their countries according to the Chinese model.

I hope that everyone in the world will understand how important public ownership of land is and that people will reach a consensus by spreading my book widely. Then people will greatly reduce the number of conflicts and make public ownership of land at low costs possible. People all over the world will reap the benefits. For example, the poor will get wealthy, and the rich will achieve security.

I hope to establish a perfect social system on earth so that everyone will receive tangible benefits, which is also the will of God.

You have put a lot of effort into writing your book, and knowing that your mission in the world is very difficult, you still have things to do. Are you willing to invest more time? Where will that strength come from?

It seems that this is a mission that is impossible to complete in the eyes of ordinary people, but in my eyes, I am just completing my mission in a planned and purposeful way. At any time, I know what I am doing and what purpose I want to achieve.

Before 2004, I was collecting materials and looking for answers to various questions.

In 2004, I wrote five important articles that saved the Communist Party when it was about to collapse. It consolidated its position economically and established a framework of state governance with the Chinese model. Moreover, I stopped Taiwan's military from purchasing six hundred billion Taiwanese dollars' worth of weapons from the United States by writing articles, and I prevented war in the Taiwan Strait.

At that time, I realized that I am a person with magic power because I can change the political trend of the world by transmitting information to people. However, I needed China to set an example and perform an experiment to verify the validity of my state governance framework theory. So I secretly transmitted information to the Chinese government over the Internet, without anyone's statement or letting anyone know, which was part of my plan.

In 2013, I set up my own website to transmit information to the world. Furthermore, I changed the political trend of the world quietly by conveying information to politicians all over the world.

After August 2014, I began to write frequent articles about Islam and the West in the hope of transmitting information and providing my suggestions to politicians around the world. Most of these politicians accepted my advice because I have magical power and the support of God. Since I was afraid that terrorists would find me and exact revenge on me, I did my work secretly. They only knew that I was writing articles to provide information and advice for them, but they didn't know what my name was or what my location was.

When North Korea decided to give up its nuclear weapons in 2018, I felt that my secret mission had been completed. I needed people all over the world to know who I was, and I needed to transmit information and provide suggestions to all the people of the world, instead of just conveying information and providing advice to a few politicians secretly through the website.

I won't mind if I have to wait even longer. If I want others to know of my existence, I will always find a way because I know that no one can replace me by doing what I should do. And the world may be destroyed if I don't do what I do. Although this world was created by God, not by me, I do not want it to be destroyed, so I have no choice but to try my best to prevent it from being destroyed.

At the same time, I hope that what I have done can maximize the meaning of my life, so I chose this challenge as if I were playing a video game.

I know I can do what I am doing at the level at which I am operating because no one can surpass my abilities. I am irreplaceable except by God. But I don't know when I will succeed. Only God knows.

In what way is your book different from other self-help books?

My book tells a true story without any fiction, and my life experience is better than any Hollywood blockbuster.

Meanwhile, my book has magical power that can change the world and the minds everyone on earth, which is something that no one else can achieve.

That's why many people are afraid of my book. They are afraid of me, afraid to hear my name, and even more afraid to see my book.

Nowadays many investors from different parts of the world are outsourcing their business to the Philippines. Are you doing the same thing? Had you planned ahead of time to come here to the Philippines to promote your book?

I don't think what I am doing is business, but the transmission of God's message, so I have different ideas from other businessmen.

The people of the Philippines were the first to invite me to spread word of my book, which was unbelievable to me.

I always thought that the Jews would come to me because I support Israel and oppose Palestine. I thought the Jews might need my support.

I always thought that Syria might accept me first because I helped them the most. I think that Americans may like me best because I made Trump president. But I never expected that the people of the Philippines would accept me first.

If you were given the chance to have your own business in the Philippines, would you seize the opportunity? What type of business would you prefer?

I don't like doing business; I just like discussing problems with others. And I have experienced many failures in business. It seems that I am able to spend money and I am unable to make money, but people around me are able to earn money. Those who have worked with me have made a lot of money and become rich. I haven't because I really don't care about money.

Since this book is for everybody, which country do you hope will make your book successful?

I hope that my book will spread to every country, and I know that my book will be successful in every country sooner or later.

Those who oppose this book will soon know how small and ridiculous they are. No one can stop me from widely distributing my book because I can bring great benefits to people all over the world.

Questions Raised by the Fourth Reporter

December 2018

Tell your readers a little about yourself—where you grew up, where you live now, where you went to school, etc. Let them get to know the personal side of you.

I was born in Xinjiang, a province in the north-west of China, in 1972. Xinjiang is very cold in winter and very hot in summer and is near Russia.

My family returned to Shanghai one after another in accordance with Chinese policies when I was in college.

I went to middle school, high school, and college in Shanghai. I graduated from Shanghai University in 1995. My major was electronic technology.

My now ex-wife and I got married in 2002. After our divorce in 2005, I didn't want anyone to bother me, so I didn't live with my parents. I lived far away from my relatives and friends—by myself—so that I could concentrate on writing this book.

I feel like I've spent most of my life writing this book. I went to study, went to work, fell in love, and got married all in order to understand, analyse, and study society and earn money to support myself.

What I've been doing with my heart and soul all my life is writing this book.

What inspired you to write this book?

When I was in junior high school, I found that my ideas were different from others, and I was absolutely right. A voice kept telling me that I was going to write a book to tell people what I thought was right. In this way I would be able to help others.

In 2004, when the Chinese government was on the verge of collapse, I wrote five articles about methods of governance that were adopted by the Chinese government as basic state policy. This helped the Chinese government get through the crisis and put China on the right track. At present, China is enjoying sound development in all areas. Its people are prosperous, its society is stable, and it is recognized by all countries of the world. All this is because I have given the Chinese government a correct guiding ideology. Those in charge have used my wisdom to develop China.

Your book talks about many things that impact the world, such as terrorism. What other topics do you discuss, and why?

I want to talk about all the problems in the world, but I start with the population problem and public ownership of land. If we can figure out these two problems, we can figure out and solve all the other problems.

1) Population problem

Now Western countries have the Yellow Maghreb movement, right-wing forces, nationalism, white supremacism, the anti-immigration movement, high unemployment, economic friction with China, and so on, all related to the population problem. The population problem is the cause of all these other problems.

Because the population of Western countries is decreasing rapidly, the aging population is becoming more and more serious. Europe brought in Muslims and blacks to supplement its shortage of labour. On the surface, the aforementioned problems are small problems, but in fact they are very serious problems which will lead to conflict between civilizations.

The decline of the Western population is caused by Western culture. It is the human rights culture that has caused the population decline in Western countries. And any civilization that fails to keep its population growing steadily will soon be destroyed. So there is a serious crisis in Western culture itself.

I have written a lot of articles related to the population problem, and I hope to help Western civilization resolve this crisis. Otherwise, not only will Western civilization remain in danger, but also the interests of white people will be seriously compromised. That's not what God wants to see happen. I hope to help the West and China solve this problem.

2) Public ownership of land

Public ownership of land is a basic precondition of China's success. It is also a basic component of the Chinese model. Private ownership of land is the root cause of why people cannot get rich.

Because I am the one who built the Chinese model, I hope to introduce the Chinese model to the world. Let the world learn the basic success of the Chinese model. Let people all over the world know what to do to really generate the greatest results.

Because the Chinese model can solve many social problems, it allows people all over the world to get rich, be safe, and be happy.

How has your religious upbringing impacted your writing?

In fact, I don't have a religious belief. I believe in science and materialism. But because I've read a lot of religious books, I can understand the intentions of the authors.

These books are indeed written by God and can give guidance to human beings in certain ways.

Because the knowledge of these books is beyond the scope of human knowledge and consciousness at the times when they were written, they couldn't have been written by humans. They could only have been written by God. It is God who directs humankind.

And I think these books are not contradictory. Buddhist scriptures, the Tao Te Ching, the Bible, the Koran, and other scriptures provide guidance to human beings in different ways.

I think people today need to learn all of God's scriptures and receive his full guidance. Human beings need to practise the comprehensive teachings of these scriptures, accept God's guidance, and accept God's law.

And I think that with all scriptures and religions, we need to learn the spirit of God's guidance rather than the specific dogma that binds us.

What were your struggles or the obstacles you had to overcome to get this book written?

The biggest difficulty I faced when I wrote this book was how to overcome my fear and pressure.

Almost all the articles in my book are antiestablishment, antitradition, antimainstream, antireligion, antiauthority, antiterrorism, antitriad, and/or anticrime.

I can honestly say that in this book, I offend and criticize everyone in the world. I have hardly ever praise anyone.

When I was writing this book, it seemed that all the people of the world would come after me with knives.

I have no wife, no children, no social security, no pension, and no health insurance. I have nearly nothing. Because of this, I feel like I could die at any moment. I'm ready to die anytime. I don't want to get a wife or children, or anyone else, involved. And any type of insurance is useless to me.

Those who oppose me are ready to kill me at any moment. I have offended all the people of the world, all the hooligans, all the terrorists, all the drug dealers, all the richest people, all the most powerful people, and all the people holding high positions. And I need to promote this book all around the world so that everyone will know that this I am the author and so that everyone can find me easily, including the people who hate me.

As I write, I think, *I'm in danger.*

But God told me that if I did not write these articles and publicize my books, many people all over the world would die and the whole world would be destroyed.

I had no choice but to write the book.

So I have felt very conflicted, very tangled up, but I had no choice, I had to go this route. And I had to finish the task because I am the only one can help you. Only I can save you.

No one but me is willing to sacrifice myself to help you out of this crisis.

No one but me has the ability to help you out of this crisis.

I have no choice.

Tell your readers about your book.

Whenever there is a major crisis, an important event, or a typical case in the world, God needs to express the views that people all over the world have about these events. God gives me inspiration, and then I write some articles about these events quickly. I put these articles on the website and then have them translated them into English and Arabic. I spread them online.

Then the political direction of these big, typical, important things that happen to human beings magically change at once, and world politics move in the direction expressed in my article.

Because God wants me to write these articles and God wants me to spread these articles, these articles represent the will of God, so they have magical power. My article can immediately change the direction of world political developments.

I recommend that my readers verify what I'm saying from this perspective.

Each of my articles is marked with the date I completed it. You can check every article I wrote and then determine what the world was like before I wrote it and what the world was like after I wrote it. After I finished writing the article, what magical changes took place in the world?

You can use this method to verify everything I have said.

My book is a collection of all my articles and my statements about certain things and ideas.

There are nearly four hundred articles in my book. Every article, every event, and every sentence I write can be verified.

I hope my readers do not blindly believe what I say or blindly oppose what I say. I hope you will verify what I say through scientific methods. Thank you.

What will your readers learn from this book?

Readers can really see the truth of the world through my book.

I always feel like that I am like the little boy who told the truth in Hans Christian Andersen's fairy tale "The Emperor's New Clothes". The little boy tells the truth that the emperor has no clothes on. And I tell the truth about the world.

I have revealed that all the superior people in the world, decent people, are actually naked. They are liars. They have been deceiving the people.

My readers, only when you truly understand the truth of the world can you make the right choices and do the right things. Only when you do the right thing can you really change your destiny. You can really find wealth, security, and happiness.

That's what I want to see happen. I have helped the Chinese people gain wealth and security. I hope to help all people of the world find wealth, security, and happiness. That's what God wants me to do.

Who is your target audience, and why?

My book is relevant to everyone on earth because all the people of the world are in trouble. Every country and every person has different troubles. I wrote this book to help all people. Different people will take different things from my book.

My book will allow everyone to see the truth about the world. My book will help all people gain wisdom so that they can improve their souls and their state of mind.

I hope everyone in the world will read my books.

If you could give only one reason to someone for reading your book, what would it be?

My book can give readers the wisdom to do the right thing and then change people's fates. In the end, my readers will receive wealth, security, happiness, and the love of God. So they should buy my book.

I recommend that readers read my articles first, which are collected in a very thin and inexpensive book. But it's the most important book. Readers should have a look at that book before deciding whether to buy other books.

What do you consider to be your greatest success in life?

I hope my book will be distributed all over the world. I hope that my book will change the world by helping all the countries of the world solve all their problems. And in the end all of us can be rich and secure and happy.

This is my greatest success and my greatest happiness. It is also the ultimate goal of everything God wants me to do.

Everyone has life lessons to learn. Tell your readers about one or two of yours and how they made you who you are today.

My grandma was the person who loved me the most and treated me with the most strictness. She give me all her property, and she beat me most of the time, but I know that my grandmother only wanted me to be a good person in this life, never a bad person.

I have been following this principle all my life: only be a good person; never be a bad person. But every person and everything I have encountered in my life has hurt me badly. But I can't hurt others or seek revenge.

What I can do is write articles and accuse all the people of the world in front of God, naming the crimes they have committed.

I want God to answer the question of why people did what they have done to me. Why do they do so many bad things?

I received an answer from God, and I included it in this book.

How important is this book for you?

I haven't done anything else in my life. All I did was complete my book, which is God's view of the human world and which represents God's new contract with humankind.

This book is also the true story of how I prevented the whole world from being destroyed by writing articles and spreading them on the Internet.

This book represents the value of my life and the meaning of my life as a person.

How did you come up with the idea for your book?

Whenever I see in the news that a major event or a typical event has happened in China or elsewhere in the world, and whenever the divine world needs to express the views of God, I have an impulse to write an article. This impulse is very strong. If I don't write the article, I will keep thinking about until I actually write it.

Now when I read articles that I've written earlier, I think they are excellent. I am amazed at myself. Why is the article I wrote so excellent?

If I were asked to throw away all my writings and write this book all over again, I feel I could not do it because I have no inspiration. I don't know what to write. Even if I were to write something, the result would be plain.

I need inspiration for my writing, and I need God to give me some sort of message.

Tell your readers anything else you want to share.

I'm sorry if my articles have offended my readers. I am not maliciously attacking people or maliciously seeking to offend people. I just hope to change people's minds and correct people's wrong ideas. I just want people to do the right thing.

I hope people will read my articles in a positive light.

Because how I express something is the only way I can say it. And it's the only way people will change their minds and realize their mistakes.

I could have written my messages to be implicit and gentle, but then they would not change people's minds at all. In order to save the world, I have used some harsh words.

It's my job, like a doctor with a scalpel cutting through a sick body. It's a job. There's no choice. I do it out of goodwill rather than malice. I am doing a good thing, not an evil thing.

Are you writing more books?

I have made relatively few comments on what has happened in the world recently because I have already commented on those things and I don't want to say the same thing over and over again. That is boring.

But I have been doing publicity recently. There are many readers and journalists who have a lot of questions to ask me.

I have written a great many articles to answer questions from readers and reporters.

I clarify my statements and provide more in-depth answers to address people's concerns, doubts, and questions. Then I collect the answers to these questions and publish them together as a new book.

ABOUT THE AUTHOR

This book describes that the God dispatches his emissary to save the world from destruction in the Age of Eschaton. Things happened are all real events.

The main figure in my book is myself – the author.
A poor man aged 45 years old living in Shanghai China.

In April, 2004, I wrote 5 articles about the reform of Chinese state-owned enterprises for the first time. Unexpectedly, the content was accepted by the government as basic policies of the SOEs and has been inherited up to now.

Since then, I am a responsible person. I want to do something for God, report to him what I see and express my ideas.

Under the calling of the God, I compose and release articles on the Internet. When the world is going to perish, I totally reverse the political tendency in all countries around the world, dispel terrorism, evil, injustice and demons, and rebuild a new order in the man's world. Readers could prove my predictions through examining the writing time and contents of my articles and drastic political changes in all countries.